Bush Theatre

THIS MIGHT NOT BE IT

by Sophia Chetin-Leuner

This Might Not Be It premiered at the Bush Theatre, London, on 30 January 2024, produced by Broccoli Arts and Jessie Anand Productions.

THIS MIGHT NOT BE IT
by Sophia Chetin-Leuner

Cast

Denzel Baidoo	Jay
Debra Baker	Angela
Dolly Webb	Beth

Creative Team

Director	Ed Madden
Set and Costume Designer	Alys Whitehead
Lighting Designer	Laura Howard
Sound Designer	Max Pappenheim
Associate Sound Designer	Sasha Howe
Stage Manager on Book	Kanoko Shimizu
Production Manager	Chloe Stally-Gibson
Casting Associate	Fran Cattaneo
Outreach Consultant	Maryam Shaharuddin

Producer	Broccoli Arts
Producer	Jessie Anand Productions
Associate Producer	Rory Thomas-Howes
Associate Producer	Bush Theatre

This production was supported using public funding by the National Lottery through Arts Council England and made possible by the kind support of Sauveur Studios (www.sauveurstudios.com) and Unity Theatre Trust.

sauveur.

Cast

Denzel Baidoo | Jay

Denzel trained at the Bristol Old Vic Theatre School. He most recently played Bukayo Saka in the West End transfer of the National Theatre's *Dear England*.

Denzel's film credits include: *The Last Swim* and *Restless*, as well as short films *Gates* (NFTS) and *Reflection* (BFI). His TV credits include: *Suspicion* (Apple TV); *Kirkmoore* (BBC); *Screw* and *Consent* (both Channel 4).

He made his stage debut in *The Nutcracker* at Bristol Old Vic.

Debra Baker | Angela

Debra Baker's television credits include: *Supacell* (Netflix); *It's a Sin, Home, Phoneshop* (Channel 4); *King Gary, Holby City, Call The Midwife, Doctors, Close to the Enemy* (BBC); *The Emily Atack Show, Coronation Street* (ITV); *The Five* (Sky); *Sliced* (UKTV).

Debra's film credits include: *Re-Awakening, Body of Water, London Road, Lie Low* and *Night Bus*.

Debra's theatre credits include: *Orlando* (Garrick); *Glacier* (Old Fire Station); *SAD* (Omnibus); *The Witchfinder's Sister* (Queen's, Hornchurch); *Big Guns* (Yard); *Home Theatre* (Stratford East); *Radiant Vermin* (Soho/ New York).

Debra has also worked in the BBC Radio Drama Company for Radio 4.

Dolly Webb | Beth

Dolly trained at Guildhall School of Music and is an Open Door Alumni.

Most recently Dolly has finished filming a pilot called *The Business of Delusion* and has been part of several independent short films. In 2022 Dolly was accepted into the Introduction to Playwriting course at the Royal Court.

Dolly is thrilled to be making her professional debut at the Bush Theatre.

Creative Team

Sophia Chetin-Leuner | Writer

Sophia is a writer and teacher from London. Her first play, *Save+Quit*, toured the UK and Ireland, becoming an Irish Times Pick of the Week and ending up at VAULT Festival, where it was published by Nick Hern Books as part of their festival highlights anthology in 2017.

Sophia received the Dalio Foundation Scholarship to study on NYU Tisch's Dramatic Writing MFA (2016-18). On returning to London, Sophia was in the Bush Theatre's Emerging Writers' Group (2019). While there she developed *This Might Not Be It*, which was shortlisted for the Women's Prize for Playwriting and longlisted for the Verity Bargate Award (2020). Her other play, *Porn Play*, was also shortlisted for the Women's Prize and the Verity Bargate Award (2022).

Sophia also writes TV and film. She was part of the BBC Writersroom (2022-23) and her TV pilot *Fix* was shortlisted for the C21 Drama Script competition (2021).

Ed Madden | Director

Productions include: *The Limit* (Royal Ballet); *Octopolis* (Hampstead); *Yellowfin* (Southwark); *A Table Tennis Play* (Underbelly, Edinburgh Fringe); *A Number* (The Other Room, Cardiff); *The World's Wife* (Welsh National Opera) and *Lemons Lemons Lemons Lemons Lemons* (Warwick Arts Centre/Edinburgh Fringe/UK tour).

Alys Whitehead | Set and Costume Designer

Alys has been an Associate Designer of Dissident Theatre and NDT Broadgate.

Her previous theatre credits include: *The Angry Brigade* (LAMDA); *Sorry We Didn't Die at Sea*, *Snowflakes* (Park); *The Retreat* (Finborough); *Lysistrata* (Lyric, Hammersmith); *SAD* (Omnibus); *Maddie* (Arcola).

Laura Howard | Lighting Designer

Laura trained at LAMDA as a recipient of the William and Katherine Longman Charitable Trust Scholarship.

Lighting Designer credits include: *Elephant, Invisible* (also 59E59), *Clutch* and *The Kola Nut Does Not Speak English* (Bush); *Salty Irina* (Paines Plough); *Faun* (Cardboard Citizens); *I F*cked You In My Spaceship* (VAULT); *Give Me The Sun* (Blue Elephant); *Juniper & Jules, SPLINTERED, curious* (Soho); *Dead Air* (Stockroom); *Moreno* (Theatre503); *Cells out* (Camden People's Theatre); *We Never Get Off At Sloane Square* (Drayton Arms); *SHUGA FIXX vsThe Illuminati* (Relish Theatre); *The Moors, Three Sisters, I Hate it Here, Sparks, Nine Night, The Laramie Project* (LAMDA).

Assistant Lighting Designer credits include: *Amadigi* (English Touring Opera); *Constellations* (Donmar/West End).

Max Pappenheim | Sound Designer

Sound designer Max Pappenheim's recent theatre includes *The Night of the Iguana*, *Cruise* (West End); *A Doll's House Part 2*, *Assembly*, *The Way of the World* (Donmar); *Henry V* (Shakespeare's Globe/Headlong); *Village Idiot* (Nottingham Playhouse/Ramps on the Moon/Stratford East); *Blackout Songs*, *Sea Creatures*, *Linck and Mülhahn*, *The Fever Syndrome*, *Labyrinth* (Hampstead); *Hamlet* (Bristol Old Vic); *The Children* (Royal Court/Broadway); *Old Bridge* (Bush, Off West End Award for Sound Design, Olivier Award for Outstanding Achievement in an Affiliate Theatre); *Ophelias Zimmer* (Royal Court/Schaubühne); *Feeling Afraid As If Something Terrible Is Going To Happen* (Bush/ Roundabout, Fringe First Award); *Crooked Dances* (RSC); *Macbeth* (Chichester); *One Night in Miami* (Nottingham Playhouse); *The Mirror Crack'd*, *Being Mr Wickham*, *The Habit of Art* (Original Theatre); *The Homecoming*, *My Cousin Rachel* (Theatre Royal Bath); *The Ridiculous Darkness* (Gate); *The Circle* (also UK Tour), *Humble Boy*, *Blue/Heart*, *The Distance* (Orange Tree); *My Eyes Went Dark* (Traverse/59E59); *The Cherry Orchard*, *A Kettle of Fish* (Yard); *Switzerland*, *Spamalot*, *The Glass Menagerie* (English Theatre of Frankfurt); *Cuzco*, *Wink* (Theatre503); *Yellowfin*, *Kiki's Delivery Service* (Southwark); *Martine*, *Black Jesus*, *Somersaults* (Finborough); *Teddy*, *Looking Good Dead*, *Toast* (national tours).

Online includes: *The System*, *Barnes' People*, *The Haunting of Alice Bowles* (Original Theatre); *15 Heroines* (Digital Theatre).

Opera and Ballet includes: *The Marriage of Figaro* (Salzburg Festival); *Miranda* (Opéra Comique, Paris); *Hansel and Gretel* (BYO/Opera Holland Park); *Scraww* (Trebah Gardens); *Carmen: Remastered* (Royal Opera House/Barbican).

Radio includes: *Home Front* (BBC Radio 4). Max is Associate Artist of The Faction and Silent Opera.

Sasha Howe | Associate Sound Designer

Sasha is an autistic sound designer and composer. Their recent work in theatre includes:

As Sound Designer: *The Two Gentleman of Verona* (CSSD); *Scroogelicious*, *Rapunzel* (Theatre Peckham). As Co-Sound Designer: *Holes* (CSSD); *Owners* (Jermyn Street). As Associate Sound Designer: *The Frontline* (CSSD). As Assistant Sound Designer: *Garbo & Me* (CSSD); *Jeffrey Bernard is Unwell* (Coach and Horses).

As various technical roles: *Matilda The Musical JR.*, *Moana JR.* (James Allen's Girls' School); *Dance of Death*, *Sarah*, *Dead Poets Live: He Do The Police In Different Voices*, *Tiger Is Coming* (Coronet).

Kanoko Shimizu | Stage Manager on Book

Kanoko is a Japanese stage manager trained in the UK. Her recent projects include:

As Stage Manager on Book: *The Interview* (Park); *Es & Flo* (workshop – Wales Millennium Centre/Kiln). As Deputy Stage Manager: *La Cenerentola* (British Youth Opera). As Assistant Stage Manager: *The Jungle Book*, *Rock Follies* (Chichester); *Medea* (@sohoplace); *The Lion, the Witch and the Wardrobe* (Gillian Lynne).

Kanoko has also worked in events, including The Friends Experience (Amsterdam), X-Games CHIBA 2023 and 2024 (Chiba, Japan), and Tokyo 2020 Olympic and Paralympic Games (Tokyo, Japan).

Chloe Stally-Gibson | Production Manager

Chloe Stally-Gibson is a freelance production manager. She is also the technical manager for ChewBoy Productions and is an associate of Zoo Co Theatre Company.

Her recent work includes: *Pass It On*, *As We Face The Sun* (Bush); *Perfect Show For Rachel* (Barbican); *Welcome Home* (Soho); *The Secretaries* (Young Vic); *Caligari* (ChewBoy Productions, winner of the 2022 Untapped Award); *Space to Be* (Oily Cart).

Maryam Shaharuddin | Outreach Consultant

A youth and community facilitator, Maryam co-creates theatre with participants in the UK and Malaysia. She has delivered workshops and performances at a range of organisations including Angel Shed, Almeida, Kiln, PositivelyUK, Coney, Bush Theatre, Company Three and the National Theatre.

Her assistant directing credits include *Daytime Deewane* (Half Moon) and *Duck* (Arcola). Joy and play are at the heart of her practice in creating inclusive, socially engaged theatre. Maryam is especially passionate about making work that celebrates and elevates the stories of Muslim Women.

Broccoli Arts | Producer

Broccoli Arts produces work for stage and page, primarily for/by/about lesbian, bisexual & queer people who experience misogyny. Founded by Salome Wagaine in 2019, now run by Eve Allin, Broccoli exists to produce theatre that has variety, ingenuity and relevance. We enable queer writers and creatives to make work that is not defined solely by identity. We aim to produce work which is enjoyable, political & theatrical.

Previous productions include *Salty Irina* (Paines Plough) and *Before I Was a Bear* (Soho/Bunker Theatre).

X: @broccoli_arts | Instagram: @broccoliarts | Website: www.broccoliarts.uk

Jessie Anand Productions | Producer

Jessie Anand Productions makes theatre and opera that is fresh and playful. Since it was founded in 2018, the company has been nominated for eight Offies and premiered six new plays.

Productions include the Offie-winning *Yellowfin* at Southwark Playhouse, the acclaimed *Pennyroyal* at the Finborough, and *Orlando*, which transferred to New York in 2023 following its success in London and Edinburgh.

The company has also produced opera and musical theatre, including *Antisemitism: a (((musical)))* (Camden People's Theatre) and *Cabildo* (Wilton's Music Hall/Arcola), and is currently working with Maz O'Connor to develop her new musical *The Wife of Michael Cleary*, which recently won the MTI Stiles and Drewe Mentorship Award.

Jessie Anand Productions is supported by Stage One.

X: @jessieproduces | Instagram: @jessieproduces | Website: www.jessieanand.com/

Rory Thomas-Howes | Associate Producer

Rory Thomas-Howes is a queer, West Midlands-born producer and writer trained at East 15 Acting School and Royal Central School of Speech and Drama. His work focuses mainly on underrepresented voices in bold new writing, and he has been longlisted for the Bruntwood Prize for Playwriting, shortlisted for the Sit Up Award, the VAULT Five and the Charlie Hartill Award, and won an Off West End Commendation and Theatre Weekly's Best of Fringe Award.

As a producer, he works both freelance and as Associate Producer to Grace Dickson Productions, working on productions such as *Lady Dealer* (Roundabout at Summerhall); *SPLINTERED* (Soho) and *Project Dictator* (New Diorama) and has produced numerous sell-out shows at venues and festivals including Soho, New Diorama, Pleasance, Sheffield and Edinburgh Fringe Festival, with runs ranging from single work-in-progress performances to extensive national tours.

Bush Theatre

We make theatre for London. Now.

Opened in 1972, the Bush is a world-famous home for new plays and an internationally renowned champion of playwrights. We discover, nurture and produce the best new writers from the widest range of backgrounds from our home in a distinctive corner of west London.

The Bush has won over 100 awards and developed an enviable reputation for touring its acclaimed productions nationally and internationally. We are excited by exceptional new voices, stories and perspectives – particularly those with contemporary bite which reflect the vibrancy of British culture now.

Located in the renovated old library on Uxbridge Road in the heart of Shepherd's Bush, the Bush continues to create a space where all communities can be part of its future and call the theatre home.

bushtheatre.co.uk

Bush Theatre

Bush Theatre, 7 Uxbridge Road, London W12 8LJ
Box Office: 020 8743 5050 | Administration: 020 8743 3584
Email: info@bushtheatre.co.uk | bushtheatre.co.uk

Alternative Theatre Company Ltd
The Bush Theatre is a Registered Charity
and a company limited by guarantee.
Registered in England no. 1221968 Charity no. 270080

THANK YOU

The Bush Theatre would like to thank all its supporters whose valuable contributions have helped us to create a platform for our future and to promote the highest quality new writing, develop the next generation of creative talent, lead innovative community engagement work and champion diversity.

MAJOR DONORS
Charles Holloway
Jim & Michelle Gibson
Georgia Oetker
Tim & Cathy Score
Susie Simkins
Jack Thorne

SHOOTING STARS
Jim & Michelle Gibson
Tim & Cathy Score

LONE STARS
Jax & Julian Bull
Clyde Cooper
Charles Holloway
Anthony Marraccino & Mariela Manso
Jim Marshall
Georgia Oetker
Susie Simkins

HANDFUL OF STARS
Charlie Bigham
Judy Bollinger
Sue Fletcher
Simon & Katherine Johnson
Joanna Kennedy
Garry Lawrence
Vivienne Lukey
Aditya Mittal
Sam & Jim Murgatroyd
Martha Plimpton
Bhagat Sharma
Dame Emma Thompson

RISING STARS
Martin Blackburn
David Brooks
Catharine Browne
Anthony Chantry
Lauren Clancy
Tim Clark
Richard & Sarah Clarke
Susan Cuff
Matthew Cushen
Kim Evans
Mimi Findlay
Jack Gordon
Hugh & Sarah Grootenhuis
Thea Guest
Sarah Harrison
Uzma Hasan
Lesley Hill & Russ Shaw
Ann Joseph
Davina & Malcolm Judelson
Mike Lewis
Lynette Linton
Michael McCoy
Judy Mellor
Caro Millington
Kate Pakenham
Mark & Anne Paterson
Stephen Pidcock
Miguel & Valeri Ramos Handal
Karen & John Seal
James St. Ville KC
Peter Tausig
Joe Tinston & Amelia Knott
Jan Topham
Evanna White
Ben Yeoh

CORPORATE SPONSORS
Biznography
Casting Pictures Ltd.
Nick Hern Books
S&P Global
The Agency
Wychwood Media

TRUSTS & FOUNDATIONS
Backstage Trust
Buffini Chao Foundation
Christina Smith Foundation
Daisy Trust
Esmée Fairbairn Foundation
The Foyle Foundation
Garfield Weston Foundation
Garrick Charitable Trust
Hammersmith United Charities
The Harold Hyam Wingate Foundation
Jerwood Arts
John Lyon's Charity
Martin Bowley Charitable Trust
The Thistle Trust
The Weinstock Fund

And all the donors who wish to remain anonymous.

If you are interested in finding out how to be involved, please visit **bushtheatre.co.uk/support-us** email **development@bushtheatre.co.uk** or call **020 8743 3584.**

THIS MIGHT NOT BE IT

Sophia Chetin-Leuner

Characters

ANGELA, *fifty-six*
JAY, *twenty*
BETH, *seventeen and a half*

Notes

A dash (–) indicates an interrupted thought or unfinished sentence.

A forward slash (/) signifies an interruption.

An ellipsis (…) suggests a loaded or pregnant pause.

This text went to press before the end of rehearsals and so may differ slightly from the play as performed.

Tuesday, 9.30 a.m.

The check-in office at a NHS Children and Adolescent Mental Health Service (CAMHS).

There are nine floors in the building, this is the fourth floor – the outpatient facility.

There are two desks crammed in the small office, both covered with papers and files stacked high like kids' forts.

There is a plexiglass window that looks out onto a waiting room scattered with kids' drawings, inspirational posters, hand sanitiser and paper masks, anti-bullying leaflets and those toys you see in waiting rooms and nowhere else.

ANGELA, *sits at the desk facing the plexiglass.*

It's hot. A cheap fan is set up in the corner, angled towards ANGELA.

ANGELA (*on the phone*). Mmm… Mmm… I know. Okay. I know. I know. Okay.

She sighs heavily.

Okay. Spell her name for me again, would you? Yeah I know how to spell Beth, Gary, I meant – M… U… Oh it's her again, is it? What's happened now?

She rummages through loads of paper on her desk.

Ah. Okay. Okay.

Found her.

She opens the file, more paper spews out.

Yeah. Yeah – okay so what's the problem? But she's almost eighteen. Well it is best to put her with the adult referrals. They won't take her yet? For god's sake. Alright but, Gary, I'm looking at her folder now and it doesn't say urgent. And right now for a standard ref you're looking at – I know. I know. All I'm saying – Gary – all I'm saying – yes I know – I know they are – I know – so what I'm saying is her birthday is in Feb so it would be better –

Meanwhile, JAY, walks up to the door that separates the office from the waiting room. He carries a plant. He has that cocky awkward energy a lot of young men have but it's a bit softer around the edges, maybe because he's nervous.

He can't get in. He taps on the plexiglass.

ANGELA *holds up a finger – 'one minute'.*

JAY *struggles with the plant. Taps again.*

ANGELA *sighs and puts the phone to her shoulder. She cranes her neck a bit to be heard through the opening at the bottom of the plexiglass.*

What time's your appointment, love?

JAY. No – um – I'm Jay?

ANGELA. Date of birth?

JAY. No no sorry, I'm Jay.

I was sent – did they not – did Gary not tell you I was coming?

He puts the plant down.

ANGELA. Ohh, Jay. (*To phone.*) I'm gonna have to call you back. The temp's just arrived.

JAY. The new – yeah, hi.

ANGELA *buzzes the door open as he's speaking. JAY struggles to pick up the plant in time and make it to the door. A little dance where he pushes and she has to buzz again.*

Eventually the door opens and JAY finds himself in the office.

ANGELA. Sorry, darling, you look so young I thought you were a patient!

JAY *politely laughs.*

He looks around the room.

JAY. So – um –

He pushes the plant onto the desk opposite ANGELA*'s (if sitting looking at their monitors, they are back to back).*

He uses the hand sanitiser by the door, then wipes the sweat off his forehead, thinks about extending his hand to ANGELA, *but decides against it.*

Nice to meet you – Angela, yeah?

He's not impolite, but has the disingenuousness of someone who hasn't been in a professional setting before and doesn't want to let it show.

I hope the plant is cool. The smell of the doctor's has always / creeped me out –

ANGELA. How old *are* you?

JAY. – and my sister said it's supposed to clean the air – uh – I'm twenty.

ANGELA. Bloody hell.

JAY, *uncomfortable but trying to be polite, inspects his new desk, which is covered in papers.*

Don't mind those, just shove them out the way.

She scoops up the papers and plonks them on her own desk.

JAY. Thank you.

That a fax machine?

ANGELA. So did Gary give you a checklist then?

JAY. Yeah. Yes.

ANGELA. Let's have a look.

JAY. Don't worry, he took me through it –

ANGELA. Gary couldn't take you through his morning commute without overcomplicating it.

She gestures for him to hand it over. He reluctantly removes a folder from his dishevelled Nike backpack and hands it to her.

Here. We. Go.

She flicks through it as if evaluating a patient.

Well, this should take you through till the end of the week. At least. You'll want to start with the discharges –

JAY. Gary said to start with the self-assessments because there are so many new referrals –

ANGELA. Gary hasn't been working here for twenty-five years now, has he?

JAY. ...I don't know?

ANGELA. Start with the discharges then give me a shout and I'll take you through the next bit. Don't be overwhelmed. It's a lot but we've been handling it.

JAY (*finding this slightly funny*). Okay.

ANGELA. Let me know if you have any questions, alright, poppet?

She swivels away from him, turning back to her monitor.

JAY. Thank you (?)

He looks at the back of her head... then around the room...

So, um, Gary also said I should make some space in here. Start with the SafeCare.

ANGELA. Mm?

JAY. He asked if I would organise the office a bit. Get rid of some of this paper. Start the online system – did he not tell you? The – the SafeCare?

ANGELA. He did, did he?

JAY. Yeah, I mean, so it would be great if you could tell me what your system is here so I can not, like, get in your way too much.

ANGELA. You're alright, love.

JAY. It shouldn't take me long. Give it a bit of order.

ANGELA. Why don't you like the smell, sweetheart?

JAY. I'm happy to – what?

ANGELA. 'The doctor's.' What's it smell of?

JAY. Oh. Um. I dunno, like, a bit sweet?

ANGELA. Huh.

JAY. It's just – Gary asked me to start with the data entry so maybe I can get going this afternoon?

ANGELA. I'd rather you didn't actually.

JAY doesn't know what to do.

JAY. …okay.

ANGELA smiles and turns back to her monitor.

JAY is about to sit down when –

Suddenly the sound of loud screams, running, glass breaking.

A car alarm goes off.

JAY runs to the window and cranks it open to peer down into the car park.

ANGELA looks annoyed by the draught.

Oh my god –

What the –

ANGELA sighs: 'not again…' She doesn't take her eyes off her screen.

He's – they're – is he okay?

ANGELA. What car was it this time?

JAY. No – a – a person just – he's smashed his –

ANGELA. He'll be fine, what car is it?

More loud screams, sounds of staff trying to restrain someone.

JAY. What is –

ANGELA. What car is it, darling? – don't make me ask again.

JAY. I dunno – a silver one – a – a – a – a Nissan?

ANGELA *smiles, relieved.*

What do we do?

She looks at him then picks up the phone.

ANGELA. Hiya –

Was it –

He okay?

Okay.

Okay then.

JAY *frantically turns between her and the window.*

Well, let me know if you need anything.

She hangs up.

He'll be alright.

JAY. He'll be alright?!

Sirens.

ANGELA. See? It's fine.

JAY. Should I go help?

ANGELA. Up to you really.

ANGELA *returns to her typing.*

JAY *glares at* ANGELA *peering at her screen and charges out the room.*

JAY. How often does this happen?

ANGELA *raises her eyebrows as if 'what's his problem?' and takes a loud sip of her tea.*

Thursday, 2.10 p.m.

ANGELA *is doing a demonstration for* JAY *at her computer. He stands behind her chair, keeping his distance.*

ANGELA. So. You get the referrals up on this log and print them –

JAY. Yep.

ANGELA. And then you sort them into urgent or standard.

JAY. *We* do that?

ANGELA. Well it's easier for the doctors that way, when it's as busy as this. And then you put the form in their folder –

JAY. And how do I find their folder?

ANGELA. Just ask me.

JAY. What if you're not here?

ANGELA. I'm not going anywhere, love. Alright?

JAY. Wouldn't it be good if you could just type in a name and their whole histories would come up? Notes / and everything.

ANGELA. And then once you've done that you put them in the right pile and Dr Kim will come down and get the urgents at around lunchtime to take it to their meeting.

That's about it I reckon. You can give it a go now.

She lets him sit in her chair.

JAY. So you know that system – SafeCare – that can actually do all / this for you.

ANGELA. Do that one there up the top –

JAY *clicks about.*

That's it.

The printer groans to life. JAY *grabs it and reads it.*

His face scrunches up in discomfort.

JAY. Ah. Wow. Urgent.

ANGELA. Let me see.

She gestures for the form.

Oh it's this girl, Beth. No she's standard referral. See. It says up here.

JAY. How?

ANGELA. Well, given that she's had blocks of time with us before, and her GP didn't assess her need as urgent.

JAY. But what about –

He gestures to the folder, horrified by the information in there.

ANGELA. We're not doctors so that's not our call. She's on the waitlist for the SARC team, too, it says there, doesn't it? We can maybe put her on CBT for trauma but that's about it really.

ANGELA *moves the file onto a larger, second pile.*

JAY. How long will a non-urgent take?

ANGELA. Oof, god knows. Six months? A year after the pandemic? Depends on lots of different things. I told Gary it was better to put her in with the adults because she'll have to start waiting all over again the minute she turns eighteen. But as if he listens to a word I say.

JAY *looks at her, incredulous.*

Don't look at me like that. Everyone in these piles needs help. We can only do what we can do.

JAY. Is that the official slogan?

ANGELA *laughs.*

ANGELA. Okay, Superman. Any other questions or are you good to get back to your discharges?

JAY. I've done it.

ANGELA. Then do the self-referrals.

JAY. Done them too.

ANGELA turns to face him.

Those Gen Z fingers, innit.

ANGELA. I'd rather you did them slowly and properly. Mistakes are hard to redo here.

She stands over him, peering at his desktop. He doesn't like her in his personal space and pulls his chair away a bit.

JAY. I got this yeah? It's not rocket science.

ANGELA smiles curtly.

ANGELA. Time for a tea then, I reckon, want one?

JAY. No thanks.

ANGELA nods, grabs her mug, and leaves.

JAY looks over his shoulder, then takes Beth's file and buries it in the urgent referrals pile.

Friday, 3 p.m.

The fan is still in the same corner but is now rotating slowly.

JAY sits reading a big textbook about occupational therapy, his leg shakes.

ANGELA is slowly moving her mouse and occasionally looks over at him. She gets increasingly annoyed by his leg shaking.

Eventually –

ANGELA. Jay?

JAY. Yep?

ANGELA. Would you – do you mind – stopping that?

JAY looks at her and realises what she's talking about.

JAY. Oh shit, sorry.

ANGELA. Thanks.

He stops.

Minutes pass.

It starts again.

Jay?

JAY. Wha–

He stops.

My bad. I don't realise I'm doing it.

ANGELA. It was in my eyeline. That's all.

JAY. Sorry. Sorry.

Do you need me to do anything – maybe I could start making some piles? Get this new system started?

ANGELA *looks at his book:* Occupational Therapy.

ANGELA. You on a training course then or what?

JAY. Applying for an apprenticeship. Got my shadowing on Wednesdays at the hospital but they want experience at a work place and I need a reference so –

ANGELA. Here you are.

JAY nods.

Gary gonna write your reference?

JAY nods.

(*Laughing.*) Well good luck with that, sweetheart. You couldn't get Gary to say something nice about you if you took his whole family to the Bahamas!

JAY bristles.

JAY. But I was thinking maybe we could switch desks at some point? I'd love to get some practice in with talking to patients, you know?

ANGELA. Why an OT?

JAY. Uh, well, I guess I really believe in a more holistic approach to healthcare.

ANGELA smiles, amused.

ANGELA. Well, good for you, love.

Suddenly a girl appears in the plexi.

She has a low energy about her.

Beth? What are you doing here?

JAY tenses.

BETH. What?

ANGELA. You have an appointment?

BETH. Yeah?

ANGELA. Okay. Hm.

Well. You know the drill.

She hands her a form, impatiently.

Fill out one of these.

BETH disappears in the waiting room, we can half see her.

She gets out a bag of crisps and eats them.

ANGELA turns to JAY.

The following is exchanged in angry whispers.

What did you do?!

JAY. Got someone some help who needed it.

ANGELA. You can't do that. That's not how it works.

BETH taps at the plexi, crisps in hand.

ANGELA and JAY jump and try to resume looking professional.

BETH looks between them like 'what is going on here?'

BETH. I need a pen.

ANGELA. Is there none in the pot?

BETH *shakes her head.*

ANGELA *sighs and gives her a pen from her desk.*

BETH *disappears.*

JAY. Clearly she was an urgent case otherwise they wouldn't have given her an appointment!

ANGELA shakes her head and goes over to a stack of folders and picks up one at random.

ANGELA. Okay. Let's see. This boy. Age thirteen. Compulsions telling him to set fire to things. When's he getting seen now?

She chucks the file down. Grabs another.

And this. Yeah. Here. This poor thing – three bouts of psychosis in the past eighteen months. Not responding to medication. Now what?

She chucks that file down too.

The system is there for a reason. And it's not the best system but it's much better than your personal opinion, okay? You're new. You're inexperienced. But if you do something like this again I'm going to have to tell Gary. And you want that reference, don't you?

JAY doesn't say anything. ANGELA picks up her phone, dials.

Your three p.m. is here. Okay.

Wednesday, 12 p.m.

The fan is gone.

ANGELA. What you having for lunch, sweetheart?

JAY gestures to Tupperware in his bag without taking his eyes off the monitor.

Your mum make you that?

JAY. No?

ANGELA. But you live with her, don't you?

JAY (*nodding and mumbling*). And my sisters.

ANGELA. Do you know how I could tell? Your shirts are always ironed. And I don't know any nineteen-year-olds who iron their own shirts. One that works here anyway.

JAY. I'm twenty.

ANGELA. Oh well excuse me!

She laughs. JAY *bristles.*

Oh come on, I'm just teasing… I'm thinking about trying that new Italian place on the corner. It's just opened and I can't for the life of me remember what was there before it. Maybe one of them kebab places but I really don't think it was, you know. I'll have to ask Nancy on my way out.

JAY. Mm.

ANGELA. Have you met Nancy yet?

JAY *shakes his head.*

Nurse down on two?

JAY. No, I haven't.

ANGELA. Oh you must meet her. Lovely girl.

JAY *grunts.*

Well, I'll try not to be too long. Maybe I'll get it to takeaway. But then I do worry about how that stuff travels. Maybe if I get a pizza I'll get it to takeaway. That way you can have a slice –

JAY. Don't worry about it.

ANGELA. But then if it's something like lasagne then I don't really want to get it in one of those cardboard containers, you know, because then it's all soggy. I do love treating myself to a nice meal out. There is just something so nice about it all being brought to you, don't you think? I'll see if Nancy wants to join, that'll be nice. What a shame you can't come too.

JAY. Someone needs to hold down the fort.

ANGELA laughs.

ANGELA. Oh you are funny, you really should meet Nancy.

The phone rings, JAY *goes to pick it up but* ANGELA *swoops in –*

Hello, Children and Adolescent Outpatient, this is Angela. How may I help?

So you'll be looking for Inpatient. I'll transfer you now.

She hits a button and hangs up.

I mean why not, right? You haven't got a girlfriend, have you?

JAY shrugs awkwardly.

You do?

JAY. No.

ANGELA blinks at him.

(*Filling the silence.*) …have you got a partner?

ANGELA. Oh no, just me! Anyway, I am *starving* so best be off. I'll let you know how it is. Are you sure you don't want anything?

JAY. I'm good.

ANGELA. Are you sure? Oh go on, you'll have some pizza. Everybody loves pizza.

JAY. It's really alright, Angela.

ANGELA. Fine, suit yourself! I'll try not to be too long.

JAY. Take as long as you need.

ANGELA. Honestly, you must meet Nancy. You two would really –

JAY. Okay!

She gets the hint.

ANGELA. So if anyone calls and you don't know what to do just tell them to call back in half an hour, okay?

JAY. I think I'll be okay.

ANGELA. Okay! Well, you never know!

ANGELA picks up some antibac wipes and leaves. JAY sighs with frustration.

Same Wednesday, 1 p.m.

JAY on the phone (his headphones) to his older sister, he's watering his plant.

JAY. She's just fucking nuts. It's like – you're not my boss, you know? We have the same job. But she's over here telling me what to do and it's just like – you're a fucking idiot, let me do this the better way. It's just exhausting. This place is a fucking mess. I don't know how I'm gonna do this for six months – yeah I know – I know. Sorry. How are you? How's Mum?

JAY sits down on his chair.

Did you give her a beta blocker? The little round ones. No not the blue – yeah. Give her one. See how that goes. I can stop by on my way to my internship. Yeah, I told you, every Wednesday I got work experience six till nine!

Sorry. Sorry. My neck hurts. How are you? Did you get the rest of your marking done –

JAY leans forward, takes a bite of his lunch and opens up solitaire on his computer.

That's great well done. Yeah. Yeah. Good good. That's good.

He plays solitaire.

Sorry yeah – I am listening – I know, sorry it's just this
woman – she's – it's a lot.

ANGELA *comes in holding a pizza box. She's about to go in
but hears –*

She's just bare annoying. I don't wanna get old. Imagine
talking that much shit about shit no one gives a shit about?
Like it's sad really, how dead you are, you know. How boring
your life gets. She can't wait for the Christmas party. Can't
stop talking about it. I'm dead.

He laughs. ANGELA *comes to the doorway.*

He swings round on his chair and sees ANGELA.

He sits up.

Sees the pizza box.

Beat.

He waves hello as if everything is okay.

Hey I gotta go talk to you later. Yeah yeah yeah. Yeah bye.
Love you.

He hangs up and closes solitaire. With a false sincerity –

How was it?

ANGELA. It was nice.

JAY. Yeah? You went with pizza then?

ANGELA. Yep.

JAY. Couldn't finish it?

ANGELA. It's for you.

She throws the pizza box on his desk. It's a little aggressive.
JAY *notices.*

JAY. Thank you! You're the best, Ange. Seriously, thank you.

ANGELA. You're welcome.

ANGELA *sits down and begins work.*

He is about to say something, but then he returns back to his screen.

Long silence.

JAY *glances over his shoulder at the back of* ANGELA's *head.*

JAY. Angela?

ANGELA. Hm?

JAY. I'm a bit stuck with these discharges. Do you think you could give me a hand?

ANGELA glances over.

ANGELA. What's the matter?

JAY. I can't figure out if they're meant to have a follow-up in one month or three.

ANGELA. If it's not in the doctor's notes, chase them. You've been doing that.

JAY. Ah right, that's it. Thank you.

Long silence.

Do you wanna know what I was just thinking?

No response. He looks out the window.

If you die what happens to your parking tickets?

What do you reckon?

ANGELA. I don't know.

JAY. I was at the hospital for my internship last week right and there was a car in the bay and it had two tickets and I was like what if that person drove themselves to hospital and then died there?

ANGELA. I've got to finish this.

JAY. Yeah, sorry, I know. Sorry.

He glances at her, worried.

By the way – that phone call – ugh – I wasn't talking about
you.

I was talking about my auntie. She's nuts. Mean to my sisters
– all that. I was just – that wasn't – I hope you didn't think
that was about you. Because it wasn't.

JAY *is looking at the back of her head.*

ANGELA. Okay.

JAY. Okay. Good.

Good.

…

So if you need anything, just let me know, yeah?

ANGELA. I'll take a tea.

JAY. You wha– okay. Okay. One tea coming right up.

ANGELA *turns to see if he's gone then goes over to his desk
and pours her cold tea in his plant.*

Tuesday 12.30 p.m.

They work in absolute silence.

The phone rings.

JAY *picks his up quickly – like it's a race.*

JAY. Hello, CAMHS this is Jay –

Hello?

Hi, slow down there for me please.

Right.

Okay. I can't quite –

Can you take a deep breath for me please?

Please.

Okay.

Deep breaths.

Okay.

Deep breaths.

ANGELA. Get their name.

JAY *frowns at her.*

JAY. It's going to be okay.

ANGELA. Get their name!

JAY. What's going on? Are you alright?

ANGELA *shakes her head and gets up, trying to take the phone from him.*

JAY *dodges.*

Can I just get your name –

JAY *bats* ANGELA *away.*

Michael. Hi Michael.

I'm Jay.

ANGELA *throws her hands up exasperated.*

Now why don't you walk me through what's going on.

ANGELA. Refer him to A&E.

JAY. And how long have you been feeling like this?

ANGELA *pulls a 'what the fuck are you doing?' face – tries to grab the phone again –*

ANGELA. Refer him to A&E or Crisis team!

JAY *motions to shh her.*

ANGELA *hurries back to her desk and writes on a piece of paper – she holds it up to* JAY.

'REFER HIM TO A&E OR NEARBY CRISIS TEAM.'

JAY *shakes his head.* ANGELA *throws up her hands, exasperated.*

JAY. I'm sorry, Michael, but Dr Meninger's in another appointment right now but why don't we talk this one out? I'm wondering if I could get your surname –

ANGELA *waves the sign.*

JAY *wheels away, turning his back on her.*

ANGELA *goes to grab the phone.*

JAY *wrestles her off, puts his hand over the receiver.*

ANGELA. Protocol is to refer patients to A&E or Crisis team immediately!

JAY. Stop! I got this.

ANGELA. No you don't. CRISIS TEAM NOW.

JAY *stands and walks away from* ANGELA, *phone cord getting tangled*

JAY. Michael, are you still with me?

Michael?

Hi.

Now why don't you walk me through how you're feeling.

No – no.

Dr Meninger isn't out of her session for another forty minutes I'm afraid.

But I'm here. I'm here. I'm Jay and I'm here.

So why don't we talk this one –

Hello?

Michael?

Hello?

Fuck.

He hangs up the phone.

He rummages in the folders, can't find him.

Michael... This is why we need a system! Fuck!

He gets up and searches more frantically. ANGELA *comes to help him.*

ANGELA. Here –

JAY *snatches the folder.*

Call the emergency contact.

JAY. I was about to!

He dials.

Hi there, is this Mrs Haidon? I'm Jay from the CAMHS –

Hi there yeah

Do you happen to know where Michael is right now?

Okay not to worry I just –

Yeah. Yeah we just got a call from him and he sounded a bit distressed –

ANGELA *shakes her head in disbelief.*

Any idea where he is?

Okay, Mrs Haidon, just calm down there for me please.

ANGELA. Stop telling people to calm down.

ANGELA *grabs Michael's folder and flicks through it.*

JAY. Okay, I'll let you know when we track him down, okay thank you.

Thank you.

Bye.

He hangs up.

ANGELA. I'm calling Dr M.

JAY. I can sort this.

ANGELA. Oh just sit down.

JAY, *shaken, sits down.* ANGELA *dials an extension.*

Hi Joan, sorry to bother you but your patient Michael just called in a state of distress. He hung up before the new guy could refer him to Crisis.

They exchange a quick look.

No, no mobile on file.

Okay.

Sorry to bother you?

She hangs up.

Charmer.

She turns to look at JAY *who is freaking out.*

Well we've contacted the parents. No other number on file. So now we just have to wait.

JAY. Wait?

ANGELA. 'Fraid so.

JAY *shakes his head*

JAY. I'm an OT – I could have handled that if you had let me.

ANGELA. Oh, you're an OT now, are you?

JAY. Training OT.

ANGELA *scoffs. She sits down and resumes work.*

Silence.

The phone rings.

JAY *jumps and picks it up.*

Hello this is Jay from CAMHS.

ANGELA *glances over.*

Yeah we can go ahead and cancel your appointment for you, Karim. Sorry you aren't feeling well. Hope to see you next week. Bye. Bye.

ANGELA *gets up.*

Where you going?

ANGELA. To get the quarterly reports from upstairs. Is that okay with you?

Same Tuesday, 2.15 p.m.

ANGELA *comes back from lunch.* JAY *has unloaded all the filing cabinets, piles of paper and folders cover the carpet.*

ANGELA. What's going on?

JAY. Stuff in these should have been processed years ago. It's just been sitting here.

He hands her a wad of papers.

Has no one wondered where these were?

ANGELA *looks a bit embarrassed and carries them to her own desk.*

ANGELA. Put it back, would you?

JAY. I'm putting them in the system. It'll be worth it.

ANGELA. Just put it back, please, love.

JAY. Oh come on. It'll be done by the –

ANGELA. No it won't. If you are reorganising it like this it's gonna take donkey's!

JAY. This is like objectively the right thing to do.

ANGELA. It's been working fine for me for twenty years, I think it's okay.

JAY. Yeah you've mentioned a few times!

ANGELA. Let's not get into this now.

JAY. I know this may seem a bit – overwhelming – but if we take it one step at a – at a –

ANGELA. Oh stop that. Take your lunch now.

JAY. Are you just gonna tidy it away?

ANGELA. Are you just gonna starve?

JAY. I brought my own lunch. I always bring my own –

He reaches down for another pile.

ANGELA. I don't like it!

JAY. I'm sorry but this is what should have been done like twenty years ago! There's patients in here that had Y2K anxiety! We need to make space!

ANGELA. Just leave it how it is!

JAY. Well if everyone just did that there would never be any progress.

ANGELA. Oh darling, there's no such thing as progress around here.

JAY. Can you stop calling me darling, please? I'm not a child.

ANGELA rolls her eyes.

Excuse me?

ANGELA. Just put everything back to where it was and let's forget about it, alright?

JAY. Even if I wanted to I can't because I don't know where everything was because there was no system here in the first place!?

ANGELA. Yes there was – it was *my* system –

JAY. What was it then? Patient's star sign? Favourite colour? Way they take their tea?

ANGELA. I'm going to report this to Gary. I'll tell him what you did earlier.

JAY. Fine – good! He knows we need a system!

ANGELA. This is *my* office.

She reaches for some papers.

JAY. No it's not.

He blocks her.

ANGELA *kicks a pile over.*

...

Are you serious?

ANGELA *grabs her bag and heads out –*

Where the hell are you going?

ANGELA (*muttering on her way out*). Bloody child telling me what to do.

JAY. Excuse me?

She's gone.

Fucking crazy bitch.

The Next Day, 9.05 a.m.

JAY *comes into the office.*

ANGELA *is wearing a witch's hat and hanging a cobweb on the plexi. It's Halloween.*

BETH *sits in the corner of the waiting room, headphones in, eating a packet of Mini Cheddars.* JAY *and* BETH *exchange a funny glance about the witch's hat.*

But then he sees the boxes are all unpacked.

JAY. Are you joking?

ANGELA. Oh, I know I look daft but the kids like it.

JAY. Where has all my work gone?

ANGELA. Oh I just gave it a little tidy.

Violation of health and safety. I almost tripped with my tea earlier.

He opens one of the cabinets. Messily stuffed with papers and files.

JAY *looks around, bewildered.*

JAY. Do you not see how weird this is?

ANGELA. It was just a bit messy, Jay. I'm sure your mum does stuff like this for you all the time.

Phone rings.

ANGELA *picks up.*

Hello, Children and Adolescent Outpatient, this is Angela.

Hi Cindy.

Hi.

Yes he is.

Yes the temp received a call from him.

Okay.

Ah, okay.

How is he?

Right.

I'll let Dr Meninger know. Okay. Thank you.

She hangs up. Doesn't say anything. JAY *gestures expectantly.*

That was Newham A&E. Michael just admitted for overdose and leg wounds. He's having his stomach pumped. Stitches. He'll live apparently. Lucky you.

JAY *exhales.*

You need to fill out one of these.

She prints a form off.

Just say patient was incoherent and you were unable to follow protocol before he hung up.

JAY *looks at* ANGELA.

He'll be fine. Go get yourself a coffee.

JAY. No thanks.

ANGELA. Refer refer refer – if the therapist is in session, refer them to nearest crisis centre to here, which is Maudsley. Failing that encourage them to go to A&E.

ANGELA *finishes pinning the cobweb up.*

BETH *finishes her packet of Mini Cheddars and maybe gets out another?*

Poor lad. We do anything to get rid of growing pains, don't we?

ANGELA *sighs, looks at the clock.*

Well I'll have a coffee, I think. Sure you don't want one?

JAY *sighs and nods, trying to keep it together.*

Ah, go on, you'll have one.

JAY *looks up at her like 'are you serious?'*

Dash of milk, yeah?

Yeah.

JAY *checks to make sure she goes. Then he shuts the door, wheeling on his seat the whole time.*

He glances at BETH. *Her headphones are in, she doesn't appear aware of what's going on.*

He quickly picks up the phone and dials an extension.

JAY. Yeah hi Gary this is Jay from outpatient fourth floor. Hiya. I'm good thanks, and you?

Ha ha…

Yeah, I'm um just wondering what the protocol is for lodging – is that the right word? – a complaint…

Yeah it is actually. She's –

She's just being –

He glances at the door. At BETH.

Am I able to come and – Thank you. Now? Okay yeah, no that's great. I'll – I'll be up in two.

He leaves.

ANGELA *comes back in with her coffee. She looks at* BETH.

ANGELA. Has the doctor not come to collect you?

BETH *shakes her head.*

I'll call up.

(*Nodding to* JAY*'s desk.*) Where'd he go?

BETH. Upstairs.

The Next Day, 5.40 p.m.

The sound of JAY*'s Dell computer shutting down.*

ANGELA *glances at him staring at the black screen. He looks exhausted.*

She considers saying something, decides against it.

She glances back, he's still staring at his black screen. She delivers most of the following to her own monitor –

ANGELA. I remember when I was in my first few months at Lewisham A&E in – too long ago – and I went out to get some lunch before an important assessment meeting or something and when I came out the shop there was this woman on a mobility scooter and she was like, 'Excuse me can you help me can you help me?' And I was like, 'Yeah, what's the problem?' And she looked really stressed, you know, and she said, 'I live just behind the station in that block of flats.' And I said, 'Okay?' And she was all 'I've got ME' or MS or – 'I can't turn the key in the lock will you help?' So I look at the time and I say, 'Okay…' even though I was a bit suspicious already at this point –

She glances over her shoulder to see if JAY *is listening. He's half-turned his head.*

But what am I gonna do, it's a little old lady? So we went and I opened the outside door to the flats and she was like, 'Thank you so much – that's my flat there,' and she had the keys at the time cos she had taken them back off me and she said it was really sticky so you just have to turn it and then like jiggle it and she gave me back the keys but – she had just opened the door! And I was like, 'You just did it, you just opened the door!' And she was like, 'No I didn't no I didn't. You might have thought it was open but it wasn't, it wasn't.' And I was thinking well this is really quite strange… So I was like, 'Okay, whatever, I'll open it but then I need to get going.' But as I was pushing it open she just started driving in behind me – on her mobility scooter – like into the flat. And it was quite narrow and she just parked it in front of the doorway so I couldn't get out! So – I was like, 'What are you doing? I need to go.' And she was like, 'Oh please don't go, I'm so lonely,' going on, 'I don't have any friends.' And I was like, 'Well I'm really sorry but – I need to go back to work, um, I've helped you and now you're not letting me leave.'

JAY *reacts – laughs, scoffs – something that shows he is listening.*

But she just sort of drove me into the kitchen and started making lunch! 'You want cheese on toast or beans on toast? Oh don't have that sandwich that's depressing,' and if I tried to leave she would wheel herself in between me and the doorway.

JAY. Why didn't you call someone?

ANGELA *turns her chair to face him.*

ANGELA. This was before mobiles. Anyway so, we ate the lunch and then she's like – oh my god I haven't thought about this in ages – then she says – she says, 'Shall we do a puzzle?'

JAY. A puzzle?

ANGELA. Yeah, and she wheeled off.

JAY. To get a puzzle?

ANGELA. Well yeah, but obviously I took my opportunity and legged it to the door but then she comes wheeling back just as I'm unbolting it and she charges at me with all these puzzles on her lap – and I'm like, 'YOU ARE HOLDING ME AGAINST MY WILL.'

She laughs, as if this is the punchline.

JAY. And then she let you go?

ANGELA. And then she let me go. And I went back to work and told my team and they were all, 'Oh does she look like this?' And I was like, 'Yeah.' And they were like, 'Oh that's Ruth, she's in here all the time she's banned from a lot of the shops because she likes to hold people hostage.'

JAY. Whoa. That's mad. Did you ever see her again?

ANGELA. Yeah, on the street. She was fine. In her sixties. Obviously unwell. But yeah it was quite a funny – scary – not terrifying – story. It's just quite a funny story.

JAY. Yeah. It is.

…

ANGELA. Well I better be off then.

She stands and gets her coat on.

JAY. Yeah me too.

She pauses at the door, wrapping her scarf around her neck.

ANGELA. But sometimes you just don't know stuff till you know stuff. You know?

A moment.

JAY. Yeah.

Thank you.

ANGELA. See you tomorrow, love. Oh sorry – Jay.

JAY gestures that it's okay. ANGELA leaves. JAY looks around the office.

Sunday, 3.40 p.m.

Sunday afternoon at the office. JAY is filing away, data-entering on his computer, wearing trackies, music blaring.

ANGELA comes in, wearing jeans.

ANGELA. What are you doing here?

JAY. I – shit sorry.

> *JAY turns the music off.*

> Sorry.

> *ANGELA looks at the neat piles.*

> Yeah – I just – thought if I did it on the weekends – out of your way – you wouldn't mind –

ANGELA. How long have you been doing this?

JAY. Just since yesterday.

ANGELA. Blimey.

> …I'm a piece of work, aren't I? Got you coming in on weekends.

> *JAY chuckles nervously, still not gauging the atmosphere.*

JAY. I like it – it's quiet.

> …My mum's down the road so I visited her then came –

ANGELA. She's at Guy's?

JAY. Yeah, it's her heart she's just had a –

> *ANGELA looks concerned/not sure if she should ask more–*

> Why are you here?

ANGELA. I was just at home, thought I'd get some work done. Maybe order some food.

JAY. I can leave.

ANGELA. No don't be silly. I'll go –

JAY. Nah.

ANGELA. Look at us, being all polite to each other.

They smile. Sheepish.

Were you playing music?

JAY. Ah no, it's okay.

ANGELA. Turn it back on.

JAY. Nah.

ANGELA. Put it on! I love music. You like music?

JAY. ... Yeah?

ANGELA. I love music.

He puts it on. It's awkward. He turns it off.

I used to be in a band.

JAY. What?!

ANGELA. Yeah, a few actually. We had one here in the building.

JAY. In *this* building?

ANGELA. Yeah. Some staff, some patients.

JAY. No you didn't.

ANGELA laughs.

What did you play?

ANGELA. Requests mostly. Fleetwood Mac. Tina Turner.

JAY. No like what instrument?

ANGELA. Oh, I sang.

JAY. You were the front man?

ANGELA. Hardly! We played at some of the parties here.

JAY. You lot love a party here.

ANGELA. Christmas, summer, I don't know there used to be a lot of parties here.

JAY. That's mad.

ANGELA. Different times.

JAY. What were you called?

ANGELA. ...The Looney Tunes.

They laugh.

God I've just barged on in here and ruined your quiet time.

JAY. No, no not at all.

...

What food were you going to get?

Sunday, 5.10 p.m.

It's dark now. They sit on the floor, surrounded by remnants of a takeaway and tinnies.

JAY. That chicken one is lush.

ANGELA. Finish it.

JAY. I can't.

ANGELA. Take it home with you.

JAY. You should.

ANGELA. Your family can have it.

JAY. No it's alright.

ANGELA. It'll just get thrown out at my end. Go on. Take it for your sisters.

She starts scraping the food into one container. He watches her.

JAY. Can I ask you something?

ANGELA. You can ask.

JAY. How come you've been here for so long?

…

I don't mean it as an insult or anything. I just – did you not
want to ever be – to do – anything else?

ANGELA. I wanted to be a psych nurse.

JAY. Oh yeah? That's cool. How come you didn't?

ANGELA *shrugs.*

No worries if you don't wanna share, sorry.

ANGELA. No it's alright, love, there just isn't much to say
really.

My mum was one. There's a photo of her up on nine.

JAY. In the display case?

ANGELA. Yeah. She's there. With the perm.

JAY. That's mad.

ANGELA. Hm.

JAY. So why didn't you?

ANGELA. You really have to care.

You care a lot, that's nice. It shows your age.

JAY. Don't say that.

ANGELA. No I'm jealous.

Like that feeling here –

She taps on her chest blade.

About five years ago this young girl died and everyone was
so upset – I mean it was very upsetting – when they are
that young – in the paper and everything. And for days the
building was in mourning. But not me. I was sitting right

there at my desk typing away like usual thinking what the hell is wrong me with why don't I feel sad? I had to sit there and mull it over – push it out like a fart. Constipated emotions! Hah!

She sips and looks at JAY, *who is frowning.*

What? You think I'm terrible?

JAY. Nah no just thinking about – constipation.

ANGELA *raises her eyebrows.*

(*Laughing.*) No not like – there's this man at my internship – at the hospital – and he's constipated.

ANGELA. Aren't you on a psych ward?

JAY. Yeah no like – like he's so afraid of failing that he never tries. But like a really bad version of it – like he was scared to take a shit in case he failed at that.

ANGELA (*nods knowingly*). Control.

JAY. Yeah – exactly. And the OT was asking him how he was doing that week and he was like yeah good but I think my tap's been shut off. And I was like oh fuck did the council turn off his water or something am I gonna have to stay late and make some calls but he went on to, like, explain and like – you know a movie that used to make you cry and you watch it again and you don't feel anything? Or like you listen to a song that used to make you feel all nostalgic and it doesn't any more or like you haven't had a crush in ages –

ANGELA. Sure.

JAY. That's it basically. He was saying his meds – or like his new stability – mean his tap's been switched off.

ANGELA. His what?

JAY. His tap. So like – he was able to go take a shit without having a meltdown but also he didn't feel anything when he put his favourite film on?

ANGELA. What a way to put it.

JAY. I know right?

They look at each other.

ANGELA. Well that's why, isn't it. That's why I didn't become a nurse. It's too hard! You can't help anyone!

JAY. I don't think that's true.

ANGELA. Well, no, okay but *a lot* of people are lost causes, aren't they? There was this guy called Bobby and he used to stand on the other side of this plexi every day and talk to me for hours. That was back when this was the inpatient floor. Wonderful man. But every day he said he was going to discharge himself and walk into traffic.

JAY. Yeah that's tough.

ANGELA. No that wasn't the problem really. It was more the fact that it was so repetitive.

God, I sound awful, don't I! Forget it!

JAY. No no go on.

If you want to.

ANGELA. Well maybe it's a symptom of something but it just felt like that is what being a psych nurse is going to be. You can't really do anything. You can't snip snip it's all better. Even if it is better, it's always got to be managed. Everyone says 'oh I can't believe you work in the cancer ward that's so thankless' but really this isn't that different.

Give us another, would you?

JAY *cracks a beer open,* ANGELA *drinks.*

But yeah Bobby passed. And I just thought – good on you, you know?

JAY. Good on you? For killing yourself?

ANGELA. Well, listen, here's the thing. Sometimes these people talk to you about their lives and what they have to do every day and it just sounds so bloody knackering. The

headaches, the voices, the intrusive thoughts and whatnot.
And when people say I want to end it sometimes you just
think yeah – bang on, to be honest with you – I'd do the same
– that sounds shit, you're in hell, everyone around you is in
hell, why don't you just go and do it?

JAY. Did you say that to Bobby?

ANGELA. Didn't have to.

She sips.

JAY. And do you feel that way?

ANGELA. Oh get out. Look at you, practising on me.

JAY. What?

ANGELA. You trying to be all therapist on me! Saving you a
fortune on interview practice, am I?

JAY. What? No!

ANGELA. Yes you are, with the voice and everything!

'Do you feel that way?'

Get out.

If you want some practice go talk to the patients. I'm fine!

JAY. I know you are.

They sip.

Sorry.

ANGELA *rolls her eyes.*

Was your mum a good nurse?

ANGELA. Oh yeah she was amazing. But you know what they
say? If you take care of people for a living, it's the last thing
you want to do when you get home. No I'm teasing. She was
alright.

JAY. Were you close?

She laughs, sips.

ANGELA. Are you and your mum close?

JAY. Not really.

ANGELA. Liar!

...

JAY. You miss her?

ANGELA. God yeah. I mean, how long's it been? Eight years ago now, I think. Was it? Yeah, Jesus.

Sort of just a bit – bit empty – what word am I looking for? But yeah sometimes I'm in the shops and I catch myself thinking 'what would Mum like for dinner?'

JAY *looks at* ANGELA.

Oh I dunno. It's a messy business.

JAY. Messy how?

ANGELA. Oh you know. Lots of different things going on up there. Stuff you can't really make sense of.

JAY *pings the can.*

JAY. I keep getting this – it's not a dream but it sort of feels like one.

ANGELA *looks over at him.*

It's like that nagging – like when you have a cup of tea that's getting cold but you're in the middle of something.

ANGELA (*chuckling*). That's good, that's clever.

JAY *smiles, bit embarrassed.*

Well, out with it.

JAY. I dunno I guess it's like... Did you ever get lost at the shops when you were a kid?

ANGELA. You what?

JAY. Like you turn around and your mum's not there any more?

ANGELA. Course.

JAY. That's what this thing is. Feel like I'm – like I've been left in the supermarket. Like I'm standing there waiting for my mum to come find me. It's dumb, don't worry.

ANGELA. Oh go on. Finish it.

JAY. Like I feel – I feel like she's there one minute and then all of a sudden you turn around and she's gone. And you're like where she go? And you try not to panic and you wait where you are like she told you to if this ever happened – did yours tell you that too yeah?

ANGELA *nods.*

And you're standing there and then you do start to panic cos like – what if she hasn't noticed you're gone? Or what if she did it on purpose? And you start thinking that maybe this was all part of some big plan to get rid of you and you're just this annoying little shit and maybe she doesn't love you and you start going through all the things you could have done to get her to stay – if you had been better behaved maybe? Eaten the dinner she cooked for you last night instead of insisting on fish fingers? Maybe if you did your homework when she asked you the first time instead of the tenth? And the reasons are now as long as your fucking shopping list and you're just there thinking – oh shit – I've been left to fend for myself right here in the veg aisle – but just as you're thinking that…

ANGELA. What happens?

JAY. I dunno really. I just sort of come to.

JAY *sips his beer, lost in thought.*

But I guess – um – the thing that keeps nagging at me is that feeling from when you're in there – that fear – that – kids don't think about it this way, I know, well, maybe they do, who knows – but that fear – that moment – where you realise there will come a time when you'll be left alone in the supermarket. You know what I mean?

I'm talking shit now, sorry, think I've had one too many.

ANGELA *wells up.*

Are you alright?

ANGELA. God, I dunno what's wrong with me, sorry.

She tries to compose herself. JAY *feels awkward.*

Sorry. Blimey. What a mess! Get a drink in me!

JAY *looks around for some tissues. He takes some off of*
ANGELA*'s desk, offers them to her.*

Thank you, lovely.

ANGELA *tries to stop crying.*

God what are you going to tell your mates about me? I work
with this batty old lady who can't keep it together.

JAY. I won't mention it to anyone.

ANGELA. You're very sweet.

JAY. Sorry.

ANGELA. It's fine!

JAY. I don't know what to say.

ANGELA. You don't have to say anything! Come on, enough of
this. I'll go for a cig, you finish your – wow, you're up to F
already. Good for you.

*She gets up and dusts herself off. He stands. Are they going
to hug?*

She pats him on the head.

Bye, darling, sorry!

She leaves.

JAY *puts the tissues back.*

Monday, 12.15 p.m.

JAY *leans back on his chair, eyeing the door. He's on the phone.*

JAY. Yeah hi it's Jay, is Gary there? Ah okay. No worries. It's just I – um – last week I made a complaint about a colleague and I'd like to – to rescind it?

ANGELA comes in. JAY *hangs up abruptly.*

Dialled Dr Sharma's extension by mistake.

ANGELA. Blimey!

JAY. Forgot something?

ANGELA. Nah it's just bloody cold out there, isn't it!

Got my sandwich.

She takes it out her bag, sits at her desk.

Mind if I –

JAY. Yeah go ahead.

She smiles as she turns the radio on.

She eats her lunch.

She hums along to the music.

JAY *resumes alphabetising and filing in front of* ANGELA *and all seems fine. The files are now stacked in neat piles. Order is forming.*

He looks at her, eating at her desk.

He feels incredibly guilty.

Why aren't you in a band any more? You're a good singer.

ANGELA. That would be embarrassing, at my age.

JAY. Why don't we get a revival of Looney Tunes for the Christmas party?

ANGELA. No.

JAY. Why not?

ANGELA. Cos the drummer and lead guitar are now at the Royal Free, the bassist killed himself two years ago and no one has heard from the sax since she was discharged in 2001!

JAY. …Sorry.

What about a choir?

ANGELA. We don't have the budget for a choir!

JAY. No, what if you join a choir?

ANGELA *shrugs*

ANGELA. Don't like meeting new people.

JAY. Yeah but they'd only be new for a few hours.

ANGELA. I don't see myself as that old lady who is in a choir.

JAY. What do you want to do then?

JAY *finishes a stack of piles, puts them on his desk and grabs another set.*

ANGELA. What do you mean 'What do I want to do'?

JAY. Once you retire.

ANGELA. That won't be for a while, mate, cool it.

JAY. No I know. I know.

ANGELA. Trying to kick me out, are you?

JAY. No no but like – if you weren't doing this, like if it was all taken away tomorrow, what would you be doing? Like do you ever think – this might not be it?

ANGELA *shrugs*.

He comes across BETH's *file. Opens it. Reads –*

He exhales heavily.

Were you here when she first came for family counselling?

ANGELA. Who?

She looks over to see what file he's reading.

Yeah, I met her mum a few times when she dropped her off for group.

JAY. Was she awful?

ANGELA. Not particularly.

JAY. Just don't know why it took so long for someone to intervene.

ANGELA. People are always intervening with that girl. She's used so many resources. She's a pain for everyone she crosses paths with if I'm being honest.

JAY. What a horrible thing to say.

ANGELA. Hah! You'll get there eventually.

JAY looks at her a bit disgusted, she is a tad self-conscious.

He puts the file on his desk and checks his email.

He swears under his breath.

Everything alright?

JAY. I'm an occupational therapist hiring an occupational therapist.

For the amount of money they cost I don't get why my wage is gonna be so fucking low.

ANGELA. For your mum?

JAY. She's being discharged tomorrow.

He looks tired.

ANGELA. Why don't you take some time off? You can always come back to this. I bet Gary would even write you a reference now –

JAY. Fuck that.

He throws his pen on his desk, gets up.

I've taken care of her for, like, almost ten years – it's time I got on with things, you know?

ANGELA. Of course, yeah, I wasn't –

JAY. Like I have done my family-obligation bit.

ANGELA. Sometimes a bit of self-preservation is what you need.

JAY. Isn't that just another word for selfish?

JAY's phone rings. He sighs, picks up.

Hi yeah just got it now – they said three hundred for the week plus – wait can you –

He puts his hand over the mouthpiece and turns to ANGELA –

One sec.

She nods 'of course'.

(*Back to his phone.*) Yeah do you think that'll be okay? If not we can say once a week and then you can come back on your lunch? It's too far for me –

He leaves. ANGELA *frowns, concerned.*

BETH *comes in.*

ANGELA. You're late.

BETH *groans.*

BETH. Why is everyone testing me today!?

ANGELA. There are lots of other people who are waiting to be seen who would show up on time, okay?

She picks up her phone and dials the extension.

BETH *nods to* JAY's *desk.*

BETH. Where is he?

ANGELA (*into phone*). Yeah she's just arrived. Okay.

BETH. He doesn't like you, you know?

She hangs up.

ANGELA. Is that right?

Dr Kim will be down – take a seat –

JAY *comes back in. Senses a weird vibe between the two women. Doesn't say anything.*

The phone rings.

ANGELA *picks up.*

Hello this is the Children and Adolescent Outpatient Serv– Oh hi. Yeah sure. Now? Okay, yeah, on way. Everything okay? Okay.

Ta.

She hangs up.

Gotta go see Gary.

JAY *(tensing)*. Did he say why?

ANGELA. Nope.

ANGELA *pulls an 'uh-oh' face and goes to leave.*

Suddenly BETH *appears at the plexi.* ANGELA *gestures for* JAY *to 'take her'.*

She leaves.

JAY. He'll be down in a minute –

BETH. Can I charge my phone please?

JAY *freezes.*

JAY. Umm.

BETH. You have a charger in there I can see it.

She leans closer to the plexi to peer into their office.

JAY *leans back even though there's a screen between them.*

Why can't I just leave it here while I'm in my session? They always let me do that. Please!

JAY. Hang on for me just a sec –

BETH. Look I'm sorry yeah but I really need my phone? It's got my card on it. How am I supposed to get home?

He wheels around and opens the door –

JAY. Angela?

Angela!

ANGELA appears at the door.

ANGELA. What is it?

JAY. Is it okay for her to charge her phone / in here while she –

ANGELA. What?

ANGELA sighs in frustration and gestures for BETH *to pass the phone through the slot.*

We're not a café, you know.

BETH *pulls a face like 'yeah I know you fucking dickhead'.*

You're welcome.

BETH (*imitating her tone of voice*). Thank you.

JAY. We won't read your messages!

BETH. What?

BETH *finds this corny and smiles a bit.*

JAY *tries to smile off the awkwardness.*

ANGELA. I've let him know you're here.

BETH *disappears.*

ANGELA *plugs the phone in to charge.*

Watch it. She likes you.

ANGELA *gets some hand sanitiser.*

Water your plant, it's looking a bit droopy.

ANGELA *leaves again, to go to Gary's office.*

JAY *rushes to the phone. Dials Gary's extension. Can't get through.*

He considers. Looks at BETH. *Considers. Then he leaves the office.*

BETH *is collected for her session.*

Empty office.

Time passes.

Fifty minutes later.

BETH *appears in the waiting room after her session.*

Sees no one is there.

Sees her phone on the other side of the plexiglass.

Taps on the glass.

BETH. Hello?

She stares at her phone, annoyed. Tired.

She looks around to see if anyone else is there.

She curls her fingers around the plexiglass and slides it back.

She reaches her arm through, trying to grab her phone.

It doesn't reach.

She jumps.

Still can't get it.

She drags the toy table over to the plexiglass so she can stand on it and reach through.

Her body is halfway into the office, her fingers inches away from her phone...

The code of the door sounds and JAY *hurries back in, zipping up his flies.*

They freeze, look at each other.

JAY. You can't be in here.

BETH. My phone –

JAY. Please step away.

BETH *clambers back down out the window.*

He waits for her to step out then hands her her phone through the partition.

BETH. I'm not contagious.

JAY. I know. It's not because of that it's the / building's policy.

BETH. I won't tell on you.

I actually won't.

JAY. That's okay –

Are you okay?

BETH. Yeah.

BETH *doesn't move.*

JAY. Are you going home now or?

BETH. Yeah. To my nan's. Gonna smoke some weed – oh! Am I allowed to say that?

JAY *smiles and nods, still a bit cold.*

JAY. Course.

BETH. Are you going home now too?

JAY *nods.*

Who do you live with? Your family?

JAY *nods again.*

How old are you?

JAY. I'm not sure if –

BETH. What so you can know everything about me and I can't even know your AGE?

…

JAY. I'm twenty.

BETH. You look younger.

JAY. Yeah I get that a lot.

BETH. When's your birthday?

JAY. Next week, actually.

BETH. You're a Sag.

JAY *smiles a bit awkwardly.*

JAY. What does that mean then?

BETH. You're adventurous.

JAY. Am I?

...it's time for BETH *to go but she doesn't make a move.*

BETH. So is this what you wanna do then?

JAY. What do you mean?

She gestures to the office.

BETH. Be an accountant.

JAY. I'm not a...

No. I – I'm training to be a therapist.

BETH. Oh my god practise on me!

JAY. Are your sessions not helping?

BETH. No they are but like he speaks way more than I swear they're supposed to. I thought I was expected to be the one who speaks but whenever he gets a chance he's off again. Can't get a word in.

JAY. Do you find what he says useful?

BETH. Why are you so nervous?! I'm not gonna do anything!

JAY. I'm sorry I don't mean / to be –

BETH. It's just annoying cos I turn eighteen soon so gonna have to stop coming here and go somewhere else which is annoying cos I'm just getting used to him.

JAY nods.

JAY. It's very disruptive, yeah.

BETH. Yeah. Same shit over and over and over really.

She taps her phone against her knuckles.

That's crazy you want to be one of them though.

JAY. Is it?

BETH. Helping sick people all day is looooong.

JAY. What do you want to do?

BETH. I'm gonna be a teacher.

JAY. That's a form of helping.

BETH. Hm but I like kids. They're fun.

JAY smiles at her. She feels a bit creeped out.

Thanks for the charge the bus is long.

JAY. To your nan's?

BETH. Yeah. It's so far for somewhere so grim. But – yeah. She's got a good-sized freezer.

BETH is embarrassed that she said this weird thing.

JAY. What?

BETH. Like, it can hold a lot, so it's good for shopping. Like, you can – never mind.

She is embarrassed.

JAY laughs with her.

JAY. Nah I get it, I get it.

She smiles like 'okay then'. She goes to leave –

Do you – do you have anyone you can talk to?

BETH looks around like… we're at a mental-health clinic.

I mean, if your therapist isn't –

BETH. I didn't mean it like that. Please don't tell him.

JAY. No. Of course not.

I just –

He hesitates then gestures for her to wait.

He leaves his office and comes around to the waiting room so they are sharing the same space.

Look. This is not – I don't know – but – but if you ever need to talk to someone, I'm here.

JAY *walks forward.* BETH *walks back.*

BETH. That's okay.

JAY *walks back.*

JAY. Would you like to take my number? Just in case?

BETH *considers.*

You don't have to use it.

BETH. Yeah okay.

JAY. Yeah? Okay. Great. It's –

BETH *unlocks her phone –*

JAY. It's 07500895504.

She types it. It's done.

Just message me so I have your number.

BETH *laughs.*

BETH. Okay.

I'm going to miss my bus if I don't –

JAY. Of course, yeah, sorry – go. Go.

She backs out the door.

Call me anytime, okay? Yeah?

Friday, 4.55 p.m.

JAY *hovers by the door in his coat and backpack.* ANGELA *still types.*

JAY. I'm going to the pub with the nurses.

ANGELA. Okay.

JAY. Do you want to come?

ANGELA. No, I'm fine.

JAY. Okay. Well. Have a good weekend.

ANGELA. You too. Have a good birthday, Jay.

　　JAY *goes to leave but stops at the threshold.*

JAY. Are you alright?

ANGELA. Yes. You?

JAY. Me? Yeah. Yeah I'm good. I'm all good.

ANGELA. Good. See you tomorrow then.

JAY. On Monday –

ANGELA. Monday. Right. Of course. Bye.

JAY. …Bye.

　　We'll be at The Red Lion. Just in case you –

ANGELA. Okay.

JAY. Okay sorry – (*He looks as if he's about to ask about the Gary meeting again – he doesn't.*)

　　Sorry. Bye.

Monday 2.45 p.m.

JAY comes in. He is distracted because his phone keeps going off – ding ding.

He ignores it and plays the messages on the office answering machine.

GARY (*on machine*). Angela it's Gary. You know I need a decision by this Friday if you want your redundancy package processed properly. Please respond to my various emails or come up and see me.

JAY turns around to see ANGELA standing there, tea in hand.

ANGELA. God he's a tactless bugger, isn't he?

She goes to sit down.

JAY. What's going on?

ANGELA. I think you know, my love. I think you very well know.

JAY. I rescinded it – I tried to rescind it – I'm so sorry.

ANGELA. Gary's been looking for any excuse to boot me out ever since the cutbacks.

Him and you very much share the 'you can't teach an old dog new tricks' belief.

Always more of a cat person, me.

She sips her tea.

JAY. Angela – I'm so sorry – I really wish – I really really regret doing it – and – and – and I tried to take it back but they wouldn't let me and it was right after you had kicked the pile and I was so angry and – that's not an excuse –

ANGELA. Just go away.

JAY. Please can I – please can I try and explain – I'm so sorry –

ANGELA. Just shut the fuck up!

JAY is shocked but then nods in respect. ANGELA sits and seems to go back to work. JAY follows her lead.

Occasionally JAY's phone dings, he sometimes picks it up to reply.

Everything okay over there?

JAY. Yep. Sorry. I'll put it on silent.

ANGELA gets up and puts a stack of papers on JAY's desk. It's pass ag.

JAY looks at her like 'what are these?'

ANGELA. The new referrals, for you to organise into what you think is the appropriately urgent or routine.

JAY. Angela, can we not be grown-ups about this?

JAY's phone dings. He glances at it.

ANGELA. Popular boy.

JAY. No – I – it's work related.

ANGELA raises her eyebrows and returns to her seat, her back to him.

His phone dings.

ANGELA, eyes still glued to her screen –

ANGELA. Oh for fuck's sake.

Fuck off.

JAY. Do you just want me to leave?

His phone dings.

ANGELA. She's back on a bloody waitlist.

ANGELA tries to contain her emotion but ends up slamming her mouse down.

JAY. Who?

Ding ding.

ANGELA. Your girl – Beth.

JAY. She's not / 'my' girl – why would you say that?

ANGELA. *Now* they've decided to put her on the adult waitlist. For fuck's sake.

Ding ding.

Turn that off would you it's doing my head in.

JAY *checks his phone, flicks it on silent.*

ANGELA *puts her head in her hands as if she has a headache.*

JAY *doesn't know what to do.*

ANGELA *stands up and grabs her bag.*

ANGELA. Going for a fag, back in five.

JAY *looks at his phone. It's vibrating.*

He stares at it for a while. It stops.

It starts vibrating again.

He groans frustratedly and picks it up.

JAY. Hi I just heard. I'm sorry. Yeah. I know. It's a lot.

I know.

Yeah.

He listens.

Yeah. But… But – I'm sorry but I'm at work now so I can't – I – I – I know, I'm sorry but I have to go, I have work. I have to go now. I'll speak to you later.

I'm sorry.

I know.

I'm sorry.

He looks as if he's about to cry.

I'm sorry.

Okay. Well. I have to get back to work now. I'm very sorry again.

Okay. Sorry. I'm hanging up now.

Okay. Bye.

Bye.

He hangs up and chucks his phone in a drawer.

He takes a deep breath to calm down and then he kicks a filing cabinet (still seated) or puts his head in his hands.

Friday, 8.45 a.m.

The empty office. ANGELA *comes in, takes her scarf off, takes her coat off.*

Puts her bag down.

Disappears.

Comes back with a tea.

Sits down at her desk. This is her dance. Every day.

She stops. Looks around the office. Surveys her castle.

Maybe she wells up. Maybe she just takes it all in.

She picks up the phone, dials an extension. Waits.

ANGELA. Hi, is Gary there?

Monday, 4.45 p.m.

JAY *and* ANGELA *type in silence.*

A small electric heater groans in the middle of the office.

JAY. God it's boiling in here do you mind turning it down a bit?

> ANGELA *ignores him.* JAY *looks at her to see if she's heard. He apprehensively wheels towards the heater and turns it down himself.*

> *Suddenly,* BETH *appears at the plexi.* JAY *sort of jumps.*

ANGELA. Hi. Have I got my wires crossed? You're not in today, are you?

BETH. I came to speak to him.

> JAY *stands up, as if fighting the urge to leave the office.*

JAY. Hi.

> *He looks at the clock. He looks at* ANGELA.

There's no more appointments today.

> BETH *rolls her eyes.*

BETH. Yeah I know.

JAY. Yeah. Course. Um –

> JAY *looks at* ANGELA *between them. He thinks about asking* BETH *to come back to the office but instead he joins her in the waiting room or perhaps he stays where he is.*

What can I help you with?

BETH. Yeah actually you can take me off the waiting list for the adult one.

JAY. I can't do that.

BETH. Why not?

JAY. I – that's not how the system works.

BETH. Can't you just change it in the computer?

JAY shakes his head.

Are you lying?

ANGELA. Excuse me –

JAY. No.

BETH. You said you'd help me.

JAY looks at ANGELA, stressed.

JAY. I know. I'm sorry.

How about we arrange to talk once a week or something?

BETH. No I don't want you I want Dr Kim.

JAY. He can't keep seeing you any more.

BETH. Why not?

JAY. Because you're an adult now – or you're going to be very soon –

BETH. Can't you just ask him though?

JAY. He – he – the doctors measure everything on the severity of the patient's symptoms. How badly you're doing. If Dr Kim was worried about you he would have set up some temporary care to bridge the gap while you wait.

BETH. But all I've got is you.

JAY doesn't know how to answer.

You're a joke.

Like –

She can't quite articulate why she's so mad. She shakes her head.

You're a joke.

Who are you giving your number out like you're some sort of paedo?

ANGELA *shifts in her seat.*

JAY. I shouldn't have done that and I'm sorry.

I've got a lot going on at the moment.

My mum –

BETH. Nah. None of that please.

Are you kidding?

You've got a lot going on at the moment?

She laughs.

Are you kidding?

JAY *shakes his head.*

You're dumb.

JAY *looks to* ANGELA *for help.*

JAY. I know.

BETH. So you can't do anything for me?

JAY *shakes his head.*

Then don't offer to, you fucking weirdo.

Grow the fuck up.

She leaves. JAY *looks at* ANGELA, *through the plexi.*

JAY. Are you going to tell?

Two Weeks Later

The office is empty. JAY *and* ANGELA *come in. Awkward.*

JAY. Well, congratulations.

ANGELA. Thank you!

She sits down, chuffed.

JAY. I guess I should start packing up.

ANGELA. Oh don't look so glum.

JAY. Are you not mad at me?

ANGELA. It's hard to be mad with twenty k worth of compensation, baby!

JAY smiles sadly and grabs an empty box. He starts filling it with stuff.

(*Leaning back on her chair.*) God the look on Gary's face when they said he was 'not credible' and 'biased'.

I will remember that look for ever.

JAY smiles sheepishly.

I forgive you.

JAY. Is that right?

ANGELA. You're young. How are you supposed to know what is professional or not in a workplace?

JAY. Yeah, how naive of me not to think that a colleague kicking over a stack of paper is actually within the bounds of professionalism!

ANGELA looks at him.

ANGELA. You did a wrong thing, Jay. I had to call it up. It's not my fault it coincided with my wrongful dismissal.

JAY looks like he is about to say something, then he stops himself and nods in shame.

JAY. Yeah.

ANGELA. I thought my testimony about you was okay actually, no?

JAY laughs angrily.

Come on, it wasn't that bad, was it?

JAY. You can't have your cake and eat it, Angela. You got your job, you got your money. You don't need me as well.

ANGELA sobers. She nods in understanding. Then she can't help herself –

ANGELA. I think Gary came off worse though, don't you think? He got schooled! 'Poor management', 'lack of oversight' – what was that one – 'prolonged discrimination aga–'

The office phone rings, JAY goes to answer but ANGELA swoops in, wagging her finger at him like 'no no not allowed'.

Hello, Children and Adolescent Outpatient. ThisisAngelahowcanIhelp?

She gestures for JAY to stop what he's doing.

Beth Murrell –

JAY looks at her, tense. ANGELA repeats the conversation so JAY knows what's happening.

She got some glue stitches, did she?

JAY's face drops.

She wants to know if that'll bump her up the waitlist. Okay.

ANGELA chuckles sadly.

Well, I can raise it with her psychotherapist but I doubt it, I'm afraid.

Yeah.

She back at home now?

Okay. Well.

ANGELA looks at her calendar.

Well, she's in on the 20th for her final. Okay.

Thank you for calling, doctor, I'll make a note for Dr Kim.

You too.

She hangs up and sighs.

JAY. Is she okay?

ANGELA. Well.

She sighs.

She'll have to be won't she.

JAY *looks a bit faint. He sits down.*

ANGELA *looks at him.*

The deadline must be coming up for the OT courses, yeah?

JAY. I'm not applying any more.

ANGELA. Since when?

JAY *shrugs and cricks his neck.*

JAY. Since –

He gestures to the phone – to Beth.

ANGELA. What about being an OT? If this is about Gary not writing you a reference there are other people who –

JAY. What's the point, right? No one gets better yadda yadda yadda.

ANGELA. Has something happened at home? Has your mum gotten worse?

He shrugs his coat on.

JAY. What? No! What are you on about? I got fired. You got me fired.

ANGELA. Because you need to learn not because –

JAY. Just – please. I – I – just give me a sec.

He leaves.

ANGELA *checks he is properly gone then tiptoes over to his computer…*

Monday 6.20 p.m.

ANGELA *waters* JAY*'s plant, watching down the hallway to see when* JAY *will come in.*

JAY *comes in with a box of folders.*

The piles of folders have halved in number.

JAY. Hello? I thought you'd be gone for the day.

ANGELA. I heard you were popping in.

JAY. Nothing gets past you does it.

   ANGELA *holds a letter. She's trying hard not to open it.*

ANGELA. You got something in the post.

JAY. Just leave it on my desk please. I've got to go do this handover thing with the system.

   He takes a look around at the office, the new order forming.

   And look – I know it's weird but some of us are going to the pub tonight for my, like, leaving drinks? If you wanted to come –

ANGELA. Open it now, would you?

JAY. What's got you all excited? I thought secret santa was at the end of the week?

   He looks at it. Then up at her.

   What did you do?

ANGELA. Open it!

JAY. Angela…

ANGELA. Don't be mad. I wrote you a reference. Open it, please!

JAY. Isn't that like fraud or something?

ANGELA. Just open it, Jay, for god's sake!

JAY. I don't want to do that any more, I told you.

ANGELA. You think that, but you do – you really do, trust me.

JAY. Just leave me alone, Angela, I don't even work here any more.

He picks up the box again and heads for the door –

ANGELA. Don't be an idiot, Jay. Don't throw it away just cos it gets a little bit hard.

JAY. A little bit hard? I spend all day taking care of people. If it's not you fucking blabbing about your mum dying twenty years ago it's my sisters or my mum having to go in or – or – whatever. And I don't even like doing it! Sick people annoy me. If that makes me a bad person then fine. I just don't want to spend my whole life taking care of people. I hate it! I don't want to help anyone any more.

ANGELA. You're just saying that cos your tap's been turned off – because of this place –

JAY. Enough with the fucking tap. It's got nothing to do with it.

ANGELA. Then what is it to do with?

JAY. I dunno, me getting fired from a fucking *temp* job? Me growing up? Me realising that it's a joke to think you can help anyone? That making a 'difference' is stupid. That caring is just – impossible and horrible and makes you so angry and tired and I'm so – I'm so bad at it!

He laughs.

ANGELA. You know that's not true. Change looks different in real life. You know that.

JAY. Whatever, Angela. Thanks for the gesture – I guess – but –

He chucks the letter in the bin and goes to leave again but can't help himself –

That was really inappropriate.

ANGELA. Inappropriate?

JAY. Yeah, an invasion of privacy. It's super-weird and creepy.

ANGELA. What you gonna do? You gonna call HR again?

ANGELA *takes the letter out the bin and offers it to him again.*

Open it.

JAY. Stop.

ANGELA. Come on.

JAY. Seriously stop.

ANGELA. Jay.

JAY. What? You gonna block me from leaving with your mobility scooter?

ANGELA *stills. This hurt. He feels bad.*

It's been nice working with you.

ANGELA *watches him go. She looks at the letter she's still holding.*

She considers, tears it open and reads.

Thursday, 3 p.m.

ANGELA *works alone.*

BETH *appears at the plexi.*

BETH. I have to fill out one of the forms cos it's my last session today.

ANGELA. Yep you do, here you are –

BETH *takes the form but doesn't move.*

Anything else you need?

BETH *shakes her head but stays where she is.*

We've got you at Melford Crescent. Is that right?

BETH. Yeah that's my nan's.

ANGELA. That better, is it?

BETH. Yeah.

ANGELA. That's good.

…

Your appointment is in a sec, love, you better fill that out.

BETH *looks at the form.*

Go on, love, there's a pen.

She passes it to her.

BETH *still doesn't move.*

She looks at JAY*'s empty desk.*

What's the matter?

BETH. Nothing.

ANGELA. Well, what you waiting for? Go fill it out.

BETH *looks between* ANGELA *and* JAY*'s empty desk.*

BETH. You lot are so shit here.

She stomps off.

ANGELA. Hey, hey, come back here a second.

BETH *turns around, eyes rolling, ready to be told off.*

Now I know this is very unfair, sweetheart. You being let down just because you're about to go and turn eighteen.

BETH. I honestly don't care.

ANGELA. Well, something tells me you actually do this time. Have I got that right?

BETH *shrugs.*

Because before you wouldn't have even shown up for these last ones, would you? But you're here… Which – well, what does that tell you?

BETH *looks at her like 'fuck do I know?'*

I reckon that says you want to change something, hm?

And that is very unfair for them to take the help away from you just when you realise you want it, and it's going to be very hard for you to be patient over the next year or so while they sort you out with another doc. But you're used to things being very unfair and hard, aren't you? That's why I reckon you'll be able to manage yourself. Is that right?

BETH *looks at her feet. Maybe a fleeting nod.*

And, Beth, look at me.

She does.

It's good you're not 'worse' by their standards, isn't it? Why would you want to be up there with all the loonies?

BETH *smiles.*

And you know if it ever does get unmanageable, you can go to A&E, okay?

BETH *nods.*

But we have you right here.

She taps the file.

And you're not going to be forgotten about. Okay?

BETH *nods.*

Good. Now stop snotting on my screen and go fill out that form.

BETH *nods at* ANGELA. *Then disappears into the waiting room.*

Friday, 9 p.m.

Sounds of the Christmas party in full swing.

The door to the office swings open and ANGELA *stumbles in. She closes the door, gets out a cig, climbs on top of her wheelie chair, opens the window and smokes out if it.*

She fans the smoke.

The door swings open and ANGELA *throws her cigarette out quickly.*

It's JAY, *he's also drunk. He sees her by the window.*

JAY. You off then? Where's your note?

   ANGELA *squeals and climbs down from her chair clumsily.*

ANGELA. Oh my god what are you doing here?

   She hurries over to him and gives him a clumsy hug, he is a bit bemused but returns it.

JAY. I do like Nancy, you're right. I'm her plus one!

   He laughs at the grown-up sounding sound of that.

   But this party is shit. You lot had me thinking it would be the night of my life.

ANGELA. Sorry to get your hopes up.

 JAY. Do you want your present now? You won't like it.

ANGELA. You still got me a present?

JAY. I was supposed to give it to you on my last day. But.

   He goes to his computer.

   Angela, meet SafeCare! Your brand-new system!

   ANGELA *looks at him blankly.*

   Gimme a patient name. Any name.

ANGELA. Michael Haidon?

   JAY *pulls a face but types it in.*

JAY. So you just type it in and – here we go.

   All those records. Right there.

ANGELA. Wow.

JAY. I know, right.

ANGELA. And it has everyone?

JAY. Yep.

ANGELA. Try Bobby – Robert Perry.

JAY looks at her – is about to say something – but types it in.

ANGELA laughs a bit.

That's mad.

She looks at the screen, absorbing his information.

Do the boy with the teeth –

JAY. Wha– oh you mean the –

He types.

ANGELA. Yes!

JAY. Oh he's being discharged?

ANGELA. Mmm. He's moving.

Oh yeah – it says there.

Wild.

A moment while she looks at the screen, quite excited.

JAY gets back up, looking pleased with himself.

JAY. Yeah it's pretty cool, right?

Will make it easier for you. I'm gonna do the same thing for this tech company who need to go paperless within the next three years.

He nods to the smoke.

Plus you can start a fire now and everything will be saved.

ANGELA. Out with the old, in with the new!

…

You know, there was never any system here. I just memorised where everything was.

It was the only way to make sure that whatever happened there was only me who could do this one thing.

They look at each other.

You know you got in.

JAY. Don't!

ANGELA. I will push you out that window before I see you spend another six months behind a computer.

JAY. Like to see you try!

ANGELA. I know you know that you need to do this.

JAY. You do, do you?

ANGELA. You could have taken the letter with you, put it in any old bin. Could have ripped it up. But you didn't.

JAY laughs.

JAY. I'm sorry if I disappointed this picture you had of me. But I can't help it if I don't wanna 'help' any more.

ANGELA. But you do, Jay.

JAY. I'm not good at it. I'm shit at helping. I'm selfish about it. Look at the complaint I made about you – what about Beth –

His voice cracks.

ANGELA. She'll be okay I think.

JAY. I – It's honestly just not for me. I'm not cut out for it. I'm not smart enough, I'm not quick enough, I'm not smart or patient or – I'm not – I don't care enough.

ANGELA hurries over to her drawer and rummages in it.

Are you about to make me fill out a self-assessment?

ANGELA finds what she's looking for and clears her throat.

What are you doing?

ANGELA. 'Jay has been working with me for just over three months but never before have I encountered such a hardworking, quick-learning, sensitive individual in my thirty-five years at the NHS.'

JAY. What –

ANGELA. 'It is my sincerest belief that he will make an
outstanding Occupational Therapist. If you worry about his
lack of experience, please take me as a case example.

I was going through the motions of life since my mother
passed and probably before that. I was sleepwalking and I
occasionally came to only to realise how unhappy I was. Jay
helped me feel better. He turned my tap back on. This young
man is more caring, more intelligent and more committed
than he knows. He has a bright future and will go on to help
hundreds more if he wants to.'

She takes a second to compose herself.

(*Trailing off, wrapping up.*) 'Thank you very much for your
time and I hope you take him into serious consideration.'

Thank you.

…

JAY. How long did that take you to write?

ANGELA. Fucking days, mate.

They laugh. JAY looks scared.

JAY. What if I'm shit?

ANGELA. You won't be.

JAY. What if I hate it?

ANGELA. Then you'll try something else.

JAY nods to himself.

You can't be afraid of taking a shit, Jay.

*It takes a second for him to realise she's talking about the
original tap guy.*

JAY. When I made that complaint you know what the HR lady
said to me?

ANGELA. What did Linda have to say for herself?

JAY. That after a certain age, you can't really change anyone's behaviour.

ANGELA *laughs sadly under her breath.*

You think that's true?

...they look at each other.

Sounds of the party.

End of play.

Acknowledgements

Thank you to the Tavistock and Portman Trust. This play is an odd love letter to you, I hope you stay open.

Thank you to Jill Tedder for sharing your stories.

Thank you to Deirdre O'Halloran and Jen Thomas for always believing in this play and to Ammar for always believing in me. Thank you to the brilliant Wiebke Green, Sarah Meadows and Ed Madden for your help in shaping it.

S.C-L.

A Nick Hern Book

This Might Not Be It first published in Great Britain as a paperback original in 2024 by Nick Hern Books Limited, The Glasshouse, 49a Goldhawk Road, London W12 8QP, in association with Broccoli Arts, Jessie Anand Productions and the Bush Theatre

This Might Not Be It copyright © 2024 Sophia Chetin-Leuner

Sophia Chetin-Leuner has asserted her right to be identified as the author of this work

Cover photography by Henri T

Designed and typeset by Nick Hern Books, London
Printed in Great Britain by Mimeo Ltd, Huntingdon, Cambridgeshire PE29 6XX

A CIP catalogue record for this book is available from the British Library

ISBN 978 1 83904 305 5

www.nickhernbooks.co.uk/environmental-policy

www.nickhernbooks.co.uk

facebook.com/nickhernbooks

twitter.com/nickhernbooks